Flower Arrangements and their Settings

George W. Smith

Flower Arrangements and their Settings

A STUDIO BOOK

The Viking Press · New York

To my Mother and Father
who encourage me in all endeavours

All photographic work,
except for illustrations of Bermudan arrangements,
by Warren Jepson & Co. Ltd, Leeds

© George W. Smith 1967
Designed by Gillian Greenwood
Published in the United States of America by The Viking Press Inc.,
625 Madison Avenue, New York, N.Y. 10022
and in Great Britain by Studio Vista Limited,
Blue Star House, Highgate Hill, London N19
Distributed in Canada by General Publishing Company Ltd
30 Lesmill Road, Don Mills, Ontario
Phototypeset in 'Monophoto' 14 pt Bembo by Bookprint Limited
Printed and bound in Holland by NV Drukkerij Koch en Knuttel, Gouda

Contents

Introduction

This book is intended for everyone who loves flowers and derives pleasure from growing and arranging them. I am grateful to Mrs Margery Fish for suggesting that Studio Vista should commission my first book. No attempt has been made to write a how-to-do-it manual, for many adequate guides of this sort already exist. Rather my aim has been to show by finished example what diverse and harmonious effects can be achieved with a little knowledge and some degree of patience.

Through the activities of flower and garden clubs the number of accomplished arrangers increases daily, and I hope that this book may help to stimulate an even broader knowledge and appreciation of this relaxing pastime.

The first two chapters show something of the background influences that have contributed to the development of flower arrangements in Britain and America. Much of this was inspired and epitomized by the late Constance Spry, whose romantic vision of urns of elegance are still dear to the hearts of many on both sides of the Atlantic.

The next chapters deal with more specific aspects of the art, such as Church flowers, which are in themselves an act of worship and a thank offering for these precious gifts. Emphasis is also placed on the selection of containers and the use of accessories, where applicable. Included too are some of my more favourite decorations such as green and dried arrangements, and also a few ideas for dining and party tables ranging from the very grand to the more informal setting. Christmas decorations find a place because they now form part of every flower arranger's repertoire. I have tried to place the main emphasis on natural materials when dealing with this somewhat abused subject.

In a later chapter the sparse and linear modern designs of today are exemplified. The post-war years fostered a more moderate use of flowers and from this evolved a style which is particularly helpful to beginners with only limited materials to work with.

In the last pages of the book I have attempted to predict future trends. The abstract designs of the future will bear less relation to natural growth and we can expect an increasing emphasis on inter-related sculptural forms within space. Our present preoccupation with muted colour blending is likely to give way to the use of strong primary accents. While one generation may decry such changes the next will accept them. The important factor is that we shall continue to seek relaxation and enrich the lives of others by self-expression within the medium of our art.

Inspiration from the past

Alas, all the castles I have, are built with air,
thou knowst. BEN JONSON

The Sitting Room of Her Royal Highness the Princess Royal at Harewood House provides an exquisite atmosphere for flowers arranged in a manner fitting to such a fine setting. Walls of soft green watered silk and superb gilded mirrors set the scene. The room contains Thomas Chippendale's elaborately inlaid furniture which follows Robert Adam's original designs for this room.

The flowers are arranged in an antique bronze tazza filled with crumpled wire netting which serves as the holder. Arching sprays of *Berberis darwinii* and green willow catkins form the outline. Bold clivia lilies, tangerine carnations and gold roses give focal interest. Narcissi 'Fortune' provide a natural transition between the outline and focal area, which is strengthened by the addition of *Arum italicum pictum* leaves and sprays of *Skimmia japonica* in creamy blossom. Some short-stemmed flowers are elevated in metal cones filled with water. The mirror with its reflection of the room enhances the total effect of the design.

The entrance hall,
Sledmere House

A pair of gilded torchières elevate arrangements of pastel-tinted flowers and dark leaves designed to enhance Sledmere House's stately entrance. Outline material consists of sweeping sprays of copper beech and *Cotoneaster salicifolia* arranged to give a flowing background to pale buff foxtail lilies and shell-pink lupins. Both the eremurus and the lupins had their tips nipped off to dissuade them from altering shape after being positioned. Greenish-white *Lilium longiflorum* and soft gold carnations give a touch of quality to the focal area, picking up the colours of the elaborately crested and crenellated moulding of the ceiling. Cream stocks and white iris help relate the arrangement to the green and gold colour scheme of the room, set against heavy drapes of oyster silk, whilst leaves of bergenia are used to conceal the metal containers. These lofty decorations frame this elegant setting and lead the eye to enjoy the sentinel terrace urn and vista of misty parkland.

A summer welcome

The Howroyde, Barkisland, a sturdy seventeenth-century English manor house, nestles amongst an upland fold of the Pennine Hills. The entrance hall with its mullioned windows and dark panelling calls for an unpretentious arrangement of bold and gaily coloured garden flowers. A copious copper fish kettle filled with wire netting holds plenty of water which is necessary for such a large group of fresh material. Tall reedmace leaves (*Typha latifolia*), sprays of plume poppy (*Macleaya cordata*) and lemon gladioli form the outline. The vivid orange daisies of *Ligularia clivorum* together with single Shasta daisy (*Chrysanthemum maximum*) and blue hydrangea give it a robust yet casual air. Deep red astilbes, silvery artemisia and trusses of an ivory floribunda rose, 'Chanelle', are used to pick up the colours in the splendid coat of arms of Charles I. This is the work of a local craftsman and it must have required some courage to display it in a predominantly Cromwellian district.

Oriental influence in the gallery—Harewood House

By keeping to simple but distinctive material a design was created which holds the eye in one of the most splendid of English rooms, rich in decoration, furniture, china and pictures, displayed against walls of coral-red flock paper.

The lovely green celadon bowl is part of the famous collection of Chinese porcelain displayed in the Gallery. It dates from the K'ang Hsi period and has neo-classical French ormolu mounts, added in the eighteenth century.

Two sweeping branches of *Magnolia denudata* create a three-dimensional frame for arum lilies and their leaves, secured on a large pinholder. The arrangement stands on an early Georgian table of black and gold lacquer which helps to balance the height of the arrangement. As each flower bud unfolds the whole will present a striking decoration in harmony with the treasures of Chinese art.

The Princess Royal's dressing room

This more intimate room was converted into a dressing room for Her Royal Highness in 1929 and is an example of 'Adam Revival' which was popular at this period. The alcoves flanking the fireplace house a collection of semi-precious carvings including amber, jade and rose quartz. These *objets d'art* inspired the flower decoration.

Small spring flowers, including narcissi, polyanthus, freesia, winter heliotrope (*Petasites fragrans*) and lachenalias, are used in an attempt to repeat the colours and textures of the ornaments. Delicate sprays of young elm and evergreen leaves create a foil in the classical triangular pattern. Note how the gilded urn and plinth produce an elegant effect linking the arrangement to the moulding of the frieze. This type of design is a good choice for the beginner in flower decoration and suits most traditional settings.

Graciousness
at Mount Pleasant

The gardens of Bermuda provide the most varied flora imaginable and the display is particularly dazzling during the early months of the year. The arrangement here was created for a wedding reception and stands on a dumb waiter in the home of the Garden Club's President. The Lowestoft china bowl holds citrous yellow and pale pink flowers with lime green and cream foliages. A flowing movement is created by the creamy pink pendant flowers of the shell plant and the green form of *Amaranthus caudatus*. Lime green fronds of nephrolepsis fern offset the more solid forms of shell pink paeonies and some beautiful white amaryllis, streaked and veined with green and pink.

The Music Room,
Sledmere House

The Music Room at Sledmere House is dominated by the portrait of Sir Richard and Lady Sykes, ancestors of the present owner, painted by Romney and framed with Robert Adam's exquisite moulding. In the foreground on a carved gaming table are arranged early summer flowers in many welcoming tints and shades of red. Note how the velvety amaryllis lilies and silky petalled paeonies capture the feeling of the costumes in the picture.

A large meat-roasting tin painted matt black filled with two-inch mesh wire netting holds ample water to nourish the flowers and leaves, previously conditioned in deep water before being arranged. By removing most of the heavy leaves from the rhododendrons a much lighter effect can be achieved. The use of a lavish profusion of flowers in a flowing design helps to offset the rigid symmetry of the room, providing a focal point of colour.

Traditional arrangements

Verily by beauty it is that we come at wisdom
MOTTO—UNIVERSITY OF WESTERN AUSTRALIA

The traditional style of flower arranging is still the most popular one for period rooms. Decorations of massed material are always suitable, but the choice of container is important. Stemmed containers are particularly useful as they enable the arranger to achieve a flowing effect as in the antique china figure used here.

The colour scheme of pastel pinks includes amaryllis, carnations, tulips and camellia buds. The creamy white *Erica arborea* forms a colour link between the container and narcissi 'Thalia'. Trails of pinkish ivy, *Hedera helix tricolor*, create a dainty outline, and clusters of pink bergenia flowers and the delicate green of *Helleborus niger* fruits introduce subtle touches of colour. These Christmas roses last a long time when they have set seed and their 'petals' have matured to this lovely shade of green, an effect sometimes missed if they are picked too soon.

Burnished tints

This oval butler's tray has been polished until its silver plate has worn through to the copper beneath which imparts a warm peachy glow. A rich and glowing medley of spring flowers are arranged in the deep tin standing on the tray which reflects their highlights. The colour scheme begins with the focal placement of brick-red amaryllis and variations on this colour are introduced by orange and apricot gerbera daisies, sprays of echeveria in flower, early forced orange lilies together with orange scarlet tulips. Unusual touches of burnished copper come from the leaves of *Mahonia japonica*, a winter tint often acquired by this princely shrub and attributed to adverse soil or climatic conditions. Scarlet laurel berries add a luscious and unusual touch of red to this rich colour scheme. The design conforms to a roughly asymmetrical triangular pattern and is a pleasing shape to follow for a low table or beneath a picture.

Classical revival

Elegant sprays of grey-green *Garrya elliptica* flowers create the outline of this design and harmonize with the unusual metal tripod. Three winged lions form the stem of the container and help to elevate the flowers arranged in a metal bowl attached to the stand. The tassel tree, as garrya is sometimes called, is one of the most beautiful winter flowering shrubs, and its pendant male catkins are reputed to have been the inspiration for Robert Adam's much copied neo-classical festoons and garlands.

Accompanying flowers include shell pink carnations, tulips 'May Blossom' with creamy-white daffodils 'Mount Hood'. The interesting recessions of *Helleborus orientalis* combine pink, green and white in blooms of fragile perfection. To the right, note the unusual hanging flower spikes of *Billbergia nutans*, their strange green-blue flowers on arching stems bursting from bright pink bracts. Like most members of the Bromeliad family, these particular flowers last a very long time.

The splendour of lilies

Lilies are one of the most distinctive of flowers for arrangements, their luminous colours and sculptured form giving them an air of refinement and quality. Bearded flag iris of wine red and gold make choice companions for these Oregon Hybrid lilies called 'Limelight'. The flowers are arranged in an alabaster chalice and foiled by brownish red *Prunus pissardii* foliage and a few leaves of *Hosta sieboldiana*.

Lady Rosse's drawing room has a high ceiling supported by Corinthian columns and framed by delicately moulded plaster work. The furnishings and general decor, reflecting her personality and interests aided by the interior designer John Fowler's inspired touch with colour, help to create a perfect setting for antique furniture and bibelots displayed against walls of palest green-grey and heavy drapes of citrus yellow corded silk. The flower arrangement, reflected in a mirror, attempts to capture this atmosphere of elegance epitomized by the gilded bird surmounting the Chippendale mirror.

Tulip time

Many arrangers regard tulips as problem flowers because of their habit of continuing to grow in water and altering their position. However, this factor can be a most pleasing feature, provided a stylized design is not required. Most bulbous flowers appreciate being arranged in shallow water after the initial deep water treatment. Always remove any white portion on the base of the stem and split it up for half-an-inch with a sharp knife.

The container is a Victorian claret-red glass lustre stand with the holes (where the crystal drops normally hang) sealed with waterproof cement. The simple chalice shape and long stem make this a pleasing choice for an arrangement of tulips. The colour scheme includes red and crimson tulips with pale green Solomon's seal and bells of *Tellima grandiflora*, backed by marbled arum and hosta leaves. Of special interest are the curious slender ribbon tulips, *Tulipa acuminata*, with reflexed petals of red, green and yellow in a striking and attractive combination.

A pannier of fragrance

This collection of fragrant spring flowers would make a charming decoration for a guest room or dressing table, as much of its appeal relies on the sweetly scented ingredients.

The sturdy Minton cherub holds a pannier of delightful little flowers including sprigs of *Daphne mezereum*, pink and white cyclamen, wine-red primroses, grape-hyacinths and white Christmas roses (*Helleborus niger*), mingled with freesias and narcissi 'Geranium'. The small hyacinths are the straw coloured variety 'City of Haarlem'. The whole colouring of wine and cream was inspired by the pendant bells of the life plant, *Bryophyllum pinnatum*, called 'Floppers' in Bermuda where it grows wild.

A small base of velvet adds balance and importance to the arrangement and protects the table from moisture accidentally spilt when attending to the daily process of adding water.

Ode to autumn

Metal containers seem especially suited to autumn flowers. This small copper tea urn with its decorative ram's head handles is among my favourites and stands on a small copper tray. The first placements, secured by wire netting, are formed by two spikes of double peach hollyhocks, a biennial that looks lovely when the heavy leaves are removed. To these are added one or two spikes of gladioli of the dainty butterfly group. The focal area consists of dahlias—spiky peach 'Preference' and apricot-orange 'Bowland'. The graceful sprays of *Atriplex hortensis alba* along with the beech were first preserved in a solution of one part glycerine and two parts hot water. It takes about three weeks to turn these leaves from green to parchment brown. A distinctive touch comes from the seed-heads of *Rodgersia pinnata superba*. The bold leaves of this moisture-loving plant strengthen the base of the design.

The Music Room—
Harewood House

Flowers seem a fitting accompaniment to music, and here they are arranged in a room perfectly suited to both. The free-flowing lines are created by the outline of balsam poplar and red-currant, and other flowers and fruit cascade over the Adam-Chippendale gilt console table in rhythmic profusion. The ivory, rose and pink of the roses, chrysanthemums, rhododendrons and carnations echo the colours of the flowery Beauvais tapestry chairs and antique Axminster carpet.

The flickering ivory candles, reflected in the mirror, link the eye with the columns of the temple in Zucchi's painting—one of four large decorative pictures of imaginary scenes. The shimmer and dazzle of the festooned chandelier repeats these points of light. The harmony of the flowers in this setting suggest the lines of Keats—'Heard melodies are sweet, but those unheard are sweeter'.

Church decorations

I love all beauteous things
I seek and adore them
God hath no better praise
And man in his hasty days
Is honoured for them.
ROBERT BRIDGES

Arranging flowers in churches is one of the most satisfying facets of this art. Many cathedrals and churches, both ancient and modern ones, provide the perfect setting for decorations created by loving hands in an atmosphere conducive to self-expression.

This illustration shows a massive decoration of mixed red flowers created for the Festival of Flowers in Westminster Abbey organized by the National Association of Flower Arrangement Societies of Great Britain to form part of the 900th Centenary Celebrations of the Abbey. One of a pair, it formed part of the nave decorations employing six such pairs in a gradual progression of colour from the Great West Door to the Nave Altar, making a dignified and impressive scheme for this magnificent building.

The container was a lead garden urn in which was placed a rigid wooden frame supporting a collection of metal cones to hold water and plant material, making it possible to elevate the flowers ten feet in height and four in width.

The Font, York Minster

This ancient font in the crypt of York's lovely cathedral church provides a unique setting for baptism flowers. The panels of the cover portray the principal characters involved in the foundation of the first Minster. It marks the traditional site of a spring in which St Paulinus baptized King Edwin in AD627 which led to the building of the Saxon church of wood.

The flowers are arranged in gently flowing designs from containers placed on a low stone wall, special thought being given to linking the colours of the flowers to those of the cover. Notice how the *Begonia rex* leaves repeat the shape and colour of the Saint's chasuble. Attention has also been given to textural interest, for example, the farinose stems of *Primula florindae* are not unlike the mealy encrustations of the Norman stonework. The ascending spires of gladioli lead the eye to flickering candles and the presiding effigy of St Peter.

The entrance hall, Bishopthorpe Palace

For seven centuries, Bishopthorpe Palace has been the seat of the Archbishops of York and is built in an ecclesiastical style befitting a Prince of the Church.

The slender alabaster vase, over three feet high and of a lovely mellow ivory colour, seems a particularly suitable container for this setting; its vine scroll handles echoing the carved capitals of the columns in the entrance hall. As the container is porous a metal bowl filled with crunched wire mesh is fitted on top to hold the flowers. Graceful sprays of berberis and honeysuckle create a flowing outline influenced by the romantic style of the 'Strawberry Gothic' arched vaulting of the stone canopy. Pale gold dahlias and chrysanthemums give focal interest, while cream carnations form a transitional link between the outline and focal area of the design. The delicate pattern of hydrangeas add contrast and their fragile china blue picks up the colour of the walls. Handsome leaves of *Ligularia clivorum* 'Othello' balance this sweeping design at its axis.

Altar flowers at St Michael and All Angels, Headingley

Narrow-necked altar vases are a familiar problem to all who struggle with these memorials week by week. Their slender shape following the pattern of ancient lily vases was originally intended to hold only one or two votive stems. Present fashion requires a fuller effect.

In this setting the carved and gilded reredos was of such ornate magnificence that a bold arrangement was needed for the flowers to hold the eye from a distance. Turning the vases upside down and standing a shallow container on top, secured by floral clay, provided the solution. Large pinholders and blocks of water-retaining plastic sponge material ('Oasis') enabled the creation of a flowing triangular design.

This method can be recommended, assuming permission has been granted, since the arranger has much more scope than he would have if working with narrow-necked vases. Provided regular attention is given to maintaining enough water, the flowers last just as long as in deeper vessels.

Wild flowers in a chapel

A country chapel is the ideal setting for wild flowers. Included in this hedgerow miscellany are yellow ragwort, foxglove flower and seed spikes, white convolvulus and campion, rosebay willowherb and cow-parsley together with wild iris and fern fronds. The latter keep well if only fronds are selected without brown spores on their undersides.

Wild flowers have a charm of their own, but do require special care in their initial preparation if they are to last. Pick only mature growth and steep in deep water, if possible overnight, before arranging them in a vessel which holds plenty of water, in this case a brass jelly pan.

The finished group stands on an old chest belonging to this tiny hexagonal chapel in beautiful Wharfedale, Yorkshire.

The State Drawing Room, Bishopthorpe Palace

Pedestal groups are one of the most effective ways of displaying flowers because they are elevated to eye level and stand free of other distracting objects.

This group reflects the colour of the carpet and the many portraits of prelates in the State Drawing Room. Red, magenta and purple may seem a daring combination, but for a Primate's reception it looks bold and welcoming.

The soaring height of gladioli, buddleia and *Atriplex hortensis* are inspired by the Gothic architecture. Spikes of *Liatris spicata* and sprays of copper beech for outline, lead into red 'Baccara' roses, carnations, dahlias and hydrangeas for focal interest. The flowers are arranged in a large baking tin and an assembly of metal cones used to extend short stems. The carved wooden pedestal, four feet in height, enables the arrangement to be seen among a large assembly of people.

An arrangement on a font

When not in use many fonts make an effective position for a flower arrangement. Early June is not a prolific time for garden flowers, which makes my first flush of climbing 'Shot Silk' roses most welcome. A delicate salmon pink in colour, it is arranged to cascade over carved alabaster giving an association of great harmony. Stately flag iris 'Edward of Windsor', a soft buff colour suffused with brown veining, prove subtle companions for the roses, a few dusky-pink carnations and coral-pink oriental poppies all blending with the creamy stone. The poppies had their stem ends seared in a flame before being steeped in deep water for some hours along with the other flowers, prior to being arranged.

Fawn grasses lend height whilst copper beach and hosta leaves provide additional background material picking up the colours of the font's marble supporting columns.

An Easter pedestal

This decoration of mixed white flowers is a suitable choice for Easter, bearing in mind the appropriate colours of the Church's year, symbolized by the changing altar frontals and vestments.

When flowers are scarce a framework of dramatic branches and ivy make a good background for arum lilies and forced lilac. The latter is particularly difficult to keep fresh and must have its stem tips crushed or split. To revive wilted blossoms recut and crush the stem tips, placing the ends only in very hot water for five minutes, while protecting the flowers from steam with tissue paper. Then immerse the entire stem in deep cold water for several hours. This treatment will revive many woody-stemmed subjects.

This attractive wooden pedestal associates well with carved church woodwork and makes a change from the more usual wrought-iron type. A deep metal bowl fitted with a large pinholder and wire netting forms the container.

Containers with character

Beauty in things exists in the mind which
contemplates them.   DAVID HUME

Having considered some of the settings for our flowers we must
also bear in mind the importance of suitable containers. Flower
arrangers rarely limit themselves to conventional vases, in fact
they usually go to considerable lengths to search out the unusual
and distinctive in order to obtain something individual. A
successful container may embrace anything beautiful which
holds water provided it possesses the added qualities of good
design and pleasing shape. When choosing, it is wise to avoid
too much surface pattern or distracting decoration.

This charming little bronze figure holds a hanging vessel,
possibly intended for incense. Early spring flowers have been
arranged in it to make a fragrant bouquet for a bedside or
writing table. All flowers are secured in moist 'Oasis' and
include the deliciously fragrant if short-lived racemes of
Mahonia japonica redolent of lilies-of-the-valley.

The Nile fantasy

An unusual container will frequently influence the arranger's choice of plant material. This Egyptian-inspired figure of white base metal has weathered to a soft grey colour after standing out of doors. Originally such items were painted to imitate bronze. The head of the figure bears a bowl decorated with twin serpents, symbolizing the Ancient Upper and Lower Kingdoms of the Nile.

The plant material relates in colour and texture to the container, and flowing drapes of *eau-de-nil* chiffon and bronze velvet have been used to suggest the movement of water. Included are *Begonia rex* leaves of metallic grey and an unusual star-shaped begonia with a reverse side of bronze and green. The silver foliage of proteas and blue-green succulents give strong focal interest strengthened by a green fruit of *Lysichitum americanum*. Brown glycerined stems of *Cyperus diffusus*, a water grass, resemble in form the papyrus of the Nile. Though not plant material, the peacock's feathers add a touch of gorgeous colour to this fantasy.

An alabaster vase

This monumental container is ideally suited to the subdued tones and sculptured forms of dried material. Made from carved alabaster it is in ten separate sections and has proved a most versatile antique shop purchase. Originally one of a pair, each section is interchangeable and several interesting variations can be evolved.

The dried material includes grey, brown and cream items of soft matt and slightly shiny textures to blend with the carved and smooth areas of the vase and add interest to the muted colour scheme. Spikes of woolly grey mullein (*Verbascum bombyciferum*) and glycerined cycas palms give slender vertical height balanced by the downward cascading cream aspidistra and wild clematis, both glycerined. This movement is anchored at the point of axis by two grey protea flowers strengthened by bay grape leaves (*Coccolobis uvifera*) and the glycerined foliage of *Viburnum rhytidophyllum*.

A Victorian épergne

Fashions in containers change, sometimes they turn full circle. This Victorian épergne was discovered in the attic, protected by an enormous glass dome. Made by a great-aunt it is a fine example of tooled leatherwork surmounted by engraved crystal trumpets, making a light-hearted and amusing conversation piece.

Originally it was intended as a table centrepiece and here the flowers and ferns are used to capture the atmosphere of that bygone era. Variegated aspidistra leaves and asparagus fern were great favourites and are now enjoying a return to popularity. The mixed white flowers include eucharist lilies, white daffodils, hyacinths and the attractive pendant urn-shaped blossoms of the lily-of-the-valley tree, *Pieris japonica*. Two different variegated leaves add interest, an attractive marbled ivy and the evergreen *Iris foetidissima variegata*. The heart-shaped hau leaves in the centre are a rich ox-blood red and repeat the colour of the heavily fringed chenille table cloth.

Art nouveau

Occasionally a container can possess enough character of its own to predetermine the way in which the arranger tackles the problem of bringing out its best qualities. This *art nouveau* double container of iridescent glass picks up and reflects the colours with which it is associated. It requires only a small quantity of material to make an interesting composition. Here the choice of colours was influenced by printed fabrics reflecting the present revival in *art nouveau* colours and designs. Lilac-pink bergenia flowers and pinky-beige bay grape leaves provide an exciting clash of colour with hanging fruits of miniature orange. Variegated oleanders were added to simulate the form of the metal leaf on the container. Dried tendrils of vine-like Chinese gooseberry (*Actinidia chinensis*) contribute movement and grace. The acid-green velvet base provides a third major colour and gives visual weight to the lower part of the composition.

A Venetian blackamoor

Pedestals of all descriptions make attractive stands for decorations helping to elevate and give added importance to the flowers and enabling the arranger to create graceful expansive lines. Pairs of carved and coloured pine blackamoor furniture were intended to hold candelabra and are almost as fashionable today as during the eighteenth century. Frequently ornately gilded and beturbaned, they are often attributed to a Venetian origin. My example stands five feet high, including the octagonal base, and is interesting because it holds a small oval tray instead of the more usual torch.

The arrangement consists of an autumn medley of dried and preserved material including beech, wild clematis, molucella and seedheads of tulips and the attractive *Allium siculum*, with rocket-shaped seed capsules. Some long trails of amaranthus show to the full their pendant form and pick up the colour of flesh-tinted roses and trusses of pink *Pernettya mucronata* berries.

The dining table, Mount Pleasant

Here is another example of something old and beautiful which is enjoying a return to favour. This silver épergne is fashioned to resemble a palm tree. Used as a table centrepiece it gives the arranger scope to go high with the flowers, well above the heads of seated diners. Long trails of fish-tailed fern, variegated chlorophytum, ivy and selaginella cascade downwards creating a cool background for lily-flowered tulips 'White Triumphator', antirrhinums, arum lilies and green-throated white amaryllis, together with some gladioli 'Green Woodpecker'. This may seem an unusual mixture, but in Bermuda all these are found out-of-doors in May, with the exception of the tulips. These were picked from my own garden and arranged the next day after travelling three thousand miles. Note the fine glass hurricane galleries still used in old Bermudan homes to protect the candle flames.

A Chinese fish

The container should never become more important than the flowers, but sometimes we have the opportunity of using something really beautiful that is in itself a work of art. This exquisite Chinese fish falls into this category. Made during the Ch'ing Dynasty, probably in the reign of the Emperor K'ang Hsi, it has a lovely fluid form and translucent glaze of a blue described as *'clair de lune'*. It received its gilded ormolu mount in eighteenth-century France. Rising from a bed of water-plants forming the base, the handle continues the line in a rococo-inspired curve. One spray of cymbidium orchids echoes this line with graceful symplicity, the cornelian red of their lips blending with the terracotta flock wallpaper. A few mottled camellia leaves are added to strengthen the unity between flowers and container.

Designs
incorporating accessories

I too will something make
And joy in the making;
Altho' tomorrow it seem
  like empty words of a dream
  remembered on waking.
ROBERT BRIDGES

Just as interior designers enjoy arranging groups of decorative objects in studied associations, so flower arrangers take pleasure in creating decorations of plant material to enhance or contrast with ornaments or possessions of special interest. This chapter is devoted to examples of this particular type of composition.

This ancient ceramic horse of the T'ang period (AD600) originally formed part of the burial trappings of a Chinese nobleman and is a dull yellowish parchment colour. Tall fronds of date palm give swerving asymmetric height and movement to the design balanced by the lower placement of dried ornamental gourds resembling in colour and texture the surface of the horse.

The Venetian-red hau leaves provide a pleasing colour contrast to the celadon-green velvet base, used to unify all these items. Both these colours are repeated in the rosettes of echeveria used to symbolize the survival of this treasure throughout the centuries.

70

Waiting for the dawn

A Swiss craftsman has used slender vertical lines and repetition of form in the design of these two graceful water fowl carved out of teak wood. Evocative of bitterns they wait, statuesque, silhouetted against the dawn. Two parallel placements of lesser reedmace, *Typha augustifolia*, repeat the lines of the birds. To the left two pale blue iris spring from a rough textured piece of driftwood, contrasting with the greens and browns, yet sharing the birds' affinity to the water.

The tall leaves are those of the greater reedmace, *Typha latifolia*, preserved in a solution of half glycerine half water. One whorl of polished *Mahonia aquifolium* is used to hide a container of water and a pinholder, its glossy texture contrasting with the weathered root which stands, together with the other items, on an oval tray of waxed acacia wood. By the understated use of only the minimum of plant material a strongly dramatic effect can be achieved.

Chinese goddess

Figurines and small ornaments are the most obvious accessories to combine with flower arrangements. They are especially effective when they have a strong character or an atmosphere of their own. Kwan Yen, the Chinese Goddess of Mercy, is a popular choice. This particular example of the deity is of carved wood and stands on a polished base also of oriental origin. The design is a simple but rhythmic grouping of aspidistra leaves, suggested by the draped folds of her gown, their durable quality and glossy surface in harmony with the polished wood. One pristine spray of white phalaenopsis orchids curves forward to follow the lower sweep of leaves, their dignified simplicity chosen to compliment the timeless grace and purity of the goddess. Two palmate leaves of *Fatsia japonica* give variation of form without detracting from the overall pattern, while the 'Chinese' Chippendale table relates the decoration to a setting with oriental affinities.

Flowers and a fan

Fans, like flowers, have often been regarded as accoutrements of gracious living and have a natural affinity when used together. Here they find an appropriate setting in a room created to enhance oriental treasures. Walls of honey-coloured raw silk with touches of aubergine and turquoise in the curtains and carpet add interesting colour compliments to this analogy of amber, gold and maroon. The outline of the decoration consists of dried stems of *Rosa sericea pteracantha*, forming a sweeping curve against the arc of the fan without obscuring its beauty. The waxy texture of lachenalias harmonizes with the container of carved soapstone, the latter made waterproof with clear varnish then filled with damp 'Oasis'. A few leaves of coral-tinted geranium and buds of *Eucalyptus globulus* extend the line of this flowing double curve arranged in the two small containers of the carving, making an intimate decoration for a bedroom or writing table.

Underwater fantasy

The medium of the flower arranger is not restricted exclusively to the plant kingdom; occasionally allied items may fit into a scheme of great beauty. This marine scene was inspired by a visit to the sea gardens of Bermuda, but could interpret any underwater fantasy.

Secured to a base of sun-bleached driftwood a lilac sea-fan—really a member of the animal kingdom—raises a delicate tracery as if from the bed of the sea. The fan forms a frame for two *Strelitzia augusta*, whose striking white and blue flowers burst from a sheath of mauvish black. Stems of pearly-grey pussy-willow catkins rise like air bubbles from elusive fish. For added interest two perfect sea eggs nestle against the fragile form of a piece of white and brown feathery coral.

This type of composition could easily be tried out with more familiar materials combed from less exotic beaches.

Flowers by candlelight

Perhaps the best association between flowers, accessories and their related settings are those which appear uncontrived as in this setting at Bishopthorpe Palace, York.

In this illustration a pair of church spikelet candlesticks flanking the decoration give height and importance to a very long table, their mellow beauty blending with the oak refectory table and old pewter used to hold the flowers for the centre-piece. An ancient embroidered stole draped across the table introduces an appropriately ecclesiastical note without detracting from the beauty of the flowers. These include trailing sprays of defoliated old man's beard, *Clematis vitalba*, with *Vitis vinifera purpurea* (the claret vine); the latter lasts well when fully mature if the woody stem tips are boiled for half a minute before the entire stem is immersed in tepid water. Festoons of green love-lies-bleeding (*Amaranthus caudatus viridis*) and green grapes give a feeling of autumn abundance mingled with gladioli, dahlias, nerines and some brilliant scarlet vallota lilies.

Flowers and a painting

Flowers arranged in direct relationship to a picture offer many interesting possibilities. This portrait of the Countess of Rosse is a striking likeness and her head is turned as if her attention has actually been caught by the flowers. Lady Rosse is herself a devoted flower arranger and she kindly consented to my creating this asymmetric decoration at Womersley Park. The flowers compliment the tones in the painting and consist of long sprays of soft pink 'Shot Silk' roses and creamy buff *Iris germanica* 'Edward of Windsor'. A few leaves of grey-green onopordum and some peach-pink 'Madam Butterfly' roses and oriental poppies give depth to the design. The flowing movement of Solomon's seal (*Polygonatum multiflorum*) repeats the movement in the grey-blue drapery of the picture, set in its frame of blue Venetian mirror glass.

Advent

Special festivities often suggest the use of an accessory to convey the spirit of the season. Christmas and Easter are particularly popular times for creating compositions that incorporate a Madonna. This is a particularly lovely example, the frosted crystal capturing and reflecting light with an inner incandescence. It is featured in a simple design with the minimum of plant material. Three tall leaves of *Yucca filamentosa* produce aspirational height behind the meditating figure, while two sprays of marbled ivy create a gently encircling line. The whole group stands on a base covered with silver metallic paper. A few pieces of jagged crystal are introduced for contrast and added interest. This decoration, with its aura of expectancy, could well be used to portray the season of Advent. It would last for several weeks if the foliage was kept fresh in a well–type pinholder concealed behind the figurine and frequently replenished with water.

Mainly foliage and fruit

Nor white nor red was ever seen
So amorous as this lovely green.
ANDREW MARVELL

This chapter is chiefly concerned with arrangements that feature foliage and fruits and it includes several good garden plants to grow for cutting. Foliage arrangements can be very beautiful, and they are most practical too, because leaves are easy to grow, fairly inexpensive to buy, and they outlive most flowers.

A winter foliage group like the one opposite will last for several weeks. It consists of tall spikes of variegated New Zealand flax (*Phormium tenax variegata*), and glossy green camellia for outline, together with aspidistra and an assortment of variegated ivies. At the centre of the design a focal point has been created with the mottled leaves of camellia, a spray of cream ivy and *Fatsia japonica* leaves. Long spears of *Iris foetidissima* give a downward movement that contrasts well with the stencilled outline of two pinnate leaves of *Mahonia japonica*. The container, converted from an old oil lamp, is a Corinthian column of polished brass with a large metal bowl attached to hold water.

Foliage beauty

All green arrangements are particularly restful both to create and to live with. This slender green bottle is fitted with a large candlecup bowl to hold water or damp 'Oasis'. The leaves are all of a durable nature and their varied forms add interest to the monochromatic scheme. Sweeping curves of broom create the flowing triangular outline together with evergreen ruscus.

Bold aspidistra leaves provide a transitional shape between the fine pointed material and the more rounded forms of the palmate fatsia leaves and the dramatic *Philodendron bipinnatifidum*. Their glossy texture relates well with the shiny surface of the bottle. Three sprays of forced guelder rose blossom (*Viburnum opulus sterile*) are introduced for contrast, their Chartreuse-green panicles picking up the colour of the smaller bottle. A drape of velvet unifies the accessories and provides a contrasting texture, absorbing light instead of reflecting it.

Variegation

Leaves with variegation are popular both with gardeners and arrangers alike for they add interest to any foliage group. They must, however, be used with restraint and in conjunction with plainer material or objects so that their fancy markings are shown off to the best advantage.

Here, tall pointed leaves of a bronze form of *Dracaena australis* are teamed with spikes of *Iris ochroleuca* and a creamy striped leaf or two of *Iris foetidissima variegata*. Curving architectural-looking leaves of cardoon pick up the grey of the pewter plate. In the centre, one flower of the uncommon green arum lily makes a focal point, foiled by two beautifully veined leaves of the hardy *Arum italicum pictum*. At the lower right, overlapping leaves of yellow and green *Hedera colchica dentata variegata* add a touch of lightness. This same colouring is taken up by the rosettes of variegated oleander.

Green flowers

Most green flowers are fascinating, especially when viewed at close quarters. In early spring the crozier-shaped stems of *Euphorbia characias* unfurl to reveal bright green flowers with a distinctive maroon eye. The five stems arranged here in a Portuguese basket associate well with the coarse-woven texture and casual air of the container.

The green clustered flowers and handsome foliage of *Helleborus argutifolius* from Corsica recommend it to every arranger's garden. The cut flowers are difficult to keep in water but their life can be prolonged if you make a shallow incision with a sharp-pointed knife all the way up the stem, then boil and soak as described on page 81.

The new growth of Chinese hawthorn, *Photina serrulata*, adds a note of glossy bronze foliage, and picks up the colouring of the dainty sprays of *Maddenia hypoleuca* used for the outline of the decoration.

Fruitful harmony

The waxy texture of this pale turquoise marble urn suggested a combination of fruits and foliage. The container is converted from an electric lamp by using a candlecup fixed in the bulb socket with floral clay. Small seedless grapes with their translucent quality give movement to the decoration and this rhythmic feeling is accentuated by arching sprays of vine tendrils, aspidistra and variegated Japanese honeysuckle. A few tall spears of lime-green iris are from the indispensable variegated sweet flag, *Iris pseudacorus variegata*. The striking shape and iridescent surface of the moss-green *Begonia rex* leaves make them choice material for the focal area. Their maroon edging picks up the colour of two garlic seedheads and contrasts with the cream ivy leaves and unripe lemons. When using heavy fruits it is advisable to wire them to a counter-balance at the back of the container so that the arrangement will not tip forward.

The joys of winter

This collection of winter gleanings relies on vivid colouring for its effectiveness. The cornucopia basket, fitted with a pottery lining, holds sprays of *Hamamelis mollis* for outline. This witch hazel from China has spider-like flowers of yellow and maroon. Trails of wild ivy have acquired, possibly as a result of mineral privation, tints of bright cornelian red veined with yellow. A few seedheads of *Iris foetidissima* were picked when mature, but still green. Gently cutting open the pods with a razor-blade exposes the striking orange seeds without causing them to scatter as they do when over-ripe. The burnished leaves of *Mahonia japonica* provide an array of orange, flame and crimson. Three smooth spoon-shaped leaves of *Bergenia beesiana* must receive special mention, for their hues of liverish red are one of winter's joys.

Mellow fruitfulness

Decorative fruits and seedheads can provide months of colour and interest during the leaner times of the year. Ornamental gourds seldom fail to arouse comment, and here a few brilliant orange and yellow specimens have been grouped round a large custard marrow on an upturned basket. If allowed to ripen thoroughly on the plant, gourds will keep for many months, sometimes drying to the colour of old ivory.

Three sprays of shiny scarlet and yellow capsicum peppers make an unusual splash of colour. These are backed by the reversed ferrous-brown leaves of *Rhododendron sino-grande*. Glycerined leaves of beech and wild clematis create the outline of the design aided by the delicate tracery of giant *Allium albopilosum* and the smaller seedheads of *Allium aflatunense*. A few translucent berries of wild bryony combine the predominant tints of orange, yellow and red.

Time to economize

During the winter months florist's flowers are most welcome but frequently lack the robust and prolific qualities of their garden counterpart. It is necessary, therefore, to rely on other items to make the most of our purchases. Five cream 'Rose-landia' roses and some beautiful double cream freezias are made to go a little further by the addition of mottled camellia and one or two green-bronze veined ivy leaves. The handsome composite foliage of *Mahonia japonica* was first given the glycerine treatment and here its deep bronze and green-brown matches exactly the colour of the Finnish bottle. The container is reminiscent of a wine jar and prompted the use of green grapes and vine-like tendrils of *Actinidia chinensis* which give rhythm to the design. Two sprays of *Eucalyptus populifolia* flower buds and three small green slipper orchids add distinctive touches to the decoration arranged in a candlecup holder.

Table and buffet decorations

The luscious clusters of the vine
Upon my mouth do crush their wine.
ANDREW MARVELL

Table decorations fall roughly into two categories, the formal, where diners are seated, and the informal, where a help-yourself type of buffet is provided. Owing to shortage of staff and changing social customs the buffet table is rapidly gaining in popularity for the hostess at home.

This magnificent formal table setting gives a retrospective view of an age of elegance. The State Dining Room at Harewood must have witnessed many much larger gatherings but here the table is laid for twelve with an exquisite assembly of silver, china and glass on a cloth of heraldic embossed white damask. The Regency-inspired candelabrum was the gift of their late Majesties, King George V and Queen Mary, to their daughter the late Princess Royal. It is surmounted by a cascading decoration of white iris, tulips, carnations and broom set clear of the flickering candles in a silver bowl filled with damp 'Oasis'.

A wedding buffet

An arrangement in white and green forms the centrepiece for this wedding reception buffet featuring *Lilium harrisii*, the emblem flower of Bermuda. Set on a cloth of white Richleaux work, the container is a crystal comport flanked by antique hurricane lights. The effect is refreshingly cool for a warm evening.

A traditional Bermudan wedding reception consists of two cakes. One is a three-tier fruit cake covered with silver leaf for the bride and surmounted by a seedling cedar tree; the other cake is a single plain cake covered with gold leaf for the groom. During the reception the newly-wed couple plant this tree with a silver trowel, to symbolize their union. The trowel, tied with ribbon, can be seen behind the decoration.

The dining room, Sledmere House

Robert Adam allowed his knowledge of ancient Greek and Roman decorative themes to influence his neo-classical designs for this elegant dining room. In the same way we can borrow from his feeling for classical form and colour for our floral decorations.

The choice of flowers was guided by the elaborate draperies of garnet-red velvet. Gerbera daisies, carnations in glowing jewel colours, green grapes and ears of unripe barley are reflected in the polished table laid with superb silver for which Sledmere House is renowned.

When creating a table centrepiece, try to work in situ thus ensuring exactly the right proportions, using for preference 'Oasis'. This method obviates the danger of stems siphoning or water spilling on the table after completion.

The dining room
at Howroyde

This opulent yet intimate dining room reflects the personal tastes of a gracious host and offers a tempting table to the guest. Mirrored wall sconces cast the dancing light of many candles over pale apricot walls, rich polished furniture and sparkling Venetian glass.

The garden flowers of August gathered together here echo the colours of the painting of Venice. Touches of acid-green foliage lend special interest to the two groups arranged in candlecups on graceful ormolu candelabra. These include *Tellima grandiflora*, Mr Bowles' golden grass (*Millium effusum aureum*), and lime and chocolate brown zonal pelargonium leaves. Green bells of *Molucella laevis* and seedhead of *Primula florindae* add grace. Below these arrangements seedless grapes spill from the grasp of winged Bacchanites.

On the table the colourful bracts of the shrimp plant, *Beloperone guttata*, combine all the tints of coral, cream and lime green found in the other flowers. The centrepiece was kept sufficiently low so as not to impede conversation and was interesting from every angle.

Buffet supper table

Informal party tables offer much greater scope to the decorator. They permit the creation of all-round or frontal effects, unrestricted by the limitations imposed by seated place settings.

The winter decoration seen here relies on a combination of dramatic lines and unusual colour blending for its effectiveness. Sweeping palm fronds form the outline, their beige colouring leading on to the brown glycerined leaves of *Fatsia japonica* and two darker brown bottles, all standing on a natural fawn tray. Pale pink carnations and tulips of the same rosy pink as the apples repeat the colour of the cloth. All these items have an arresting diagonal movement which is visually stimulating. The parallel placement of slender tapered candles, used to stabilize the asymmetry of the design, adds a festive touch. Their prune-purple colouring supplies a distinctive offbeat colour in contrast to the browns and pinks featured in this sophisticated decoration for an evening buffet.

In the kitchen

This still-life group suggests a spontaneous kitchen get-together. Arranged on a large chopping board of scrubbed wood, the fruit and vegetables are both decorative and utilitarian. An explosive upright line is created by horned wheat and forced rhubarb secured on a pin-holder. The rhubarb with pink stems and lime-yellow leaves, was first stiffened in water. An orange quash and three green artichokes give a sculptured stability at the centre of the arrangement together with two raffia-covered bottles suggesting a party theme. The lobster, previously cooked, cleaned and reassembled gives a note of exciting colour without any attendant odour. Brown chestnuts and fawn garlic pick up the neutral tones of the board and wheat, while a solitary lemon echoes the colour of the dyed yellow okra pods and rhubarb foliage. A subtle association of crustaceous form links the lobster claws, seed pods and whiskery wheat. Placed on a cloth of coarse green linen the composition provides a colourful talking point.

A harvest supper

This harvest or thanksgiving supper table combines the earthy textures and rugged outlines of plant material associated with an autumn garnering celebration. Arranged on an old copper ashet, a decorative form of indian sweet corn, *Zea japonica variegata*, supplies variegated leaves, flowers and fruits. The striking inflorescence of the male flowers rises above the silky tassel of the female flower seen to the left of an allium seedhead. Ripened cobs burst from their papery sheaths to reveal exciting shiny seeds of gunmetal grey and bronze red. The dark crinkled leaves of ruby Swiss chard contrast well with a head of decorative white and green cabbage. Purple turnips and a few apples lead the eye to the copper ale muller and kettle. The table napkins and cloth of orange and grey-checked linen pick up the mellow colours of the old polished copper. White-washed walls, and a corn dolly worked by a friend, suggest a rustic setting.

In the Flemish manner

The art of decorating tables with flowers has been practised throughout many centuries, though our knowledge of what was used is often based only on fragmentary evidence. During the seventeenth century the prosperous Lowlands fostered the work of great painters. Particularly notable are their still-life compositions, rich in the varied juxtaposing of flowers and fruits, together with beautiful objects of metal, shell, glass and other naturalistic accessories. This has preserved for posterity a magnificent record of the flora and habits of those times.

To attempt slavishly to copy one of these paintings would result in a nugatory exercise, quite apart from the near impossibility of such a task owing to modern hybridization. Rather we should let their general freedom of composition inspire our own efforts. In making this decoration on an old table, the idea was to capture something of the casual grace of these paintings and to forget some of the so-called present-day rules.

Plant arrangements

Gr-r-r—there go, my heart's abhorrence!
Water your damned flower-pots, do!
ROBERT BROWNING

Growing green plants indoors was a favourite pastime of the Victorian and Edwardian eras. It is also a popular solution to the present-day problems created by central heating where cut flowers are short lived and costly to replenish frequently. This chapter deals with some suggestions for *pot et fleur* groups.

My large community of plants stands on an old chest and has flourished in this brass jelly pan for over three years. The green ovate leaves of the tall rubber tree, *Ficus doescheri*, are splashed and edged with cream like those of the pepper plant, *Peperomia magnoliaefolia*, seen near the rim of the container. To the left, the trailing kangaroo vine, *Cissus antarctica*, is almost indestructible and flourishes in this shady corner along with ivies, palm and *Fatsia japonica*. A coral-pink cineraria was added to give a gay touch of colour matching exactly the wild silk curtains.

Pot et fleur at Rycliffe

This attractive room provides a perfect setting for antique furniture and abstract paintings. In the same way the plant arrangement combines old favourites with quite modern-looking flowers. The plants are taken out of their pots and packed tightly with moist moss in the brass dish, care being taken to select contrasting forms and colours yet plants with similar cultural preferences. This assortment includes the variegated spider plant, *Chlorophytum comosum variegatum*, which throws out attractive hanging plantlets and on the right the feathery maidenhair fern, *Adiantum cuneatum*. In the centre a sturdy member of the pineapple family, *Vriesia splendens*, likes to have its central funnel of leaves filled up with water. Behind these rise the tough spears of variegated snake plant, *Sansevieria trifasciata laurentii* a most durable plant if not over-watered. The Bird of Paradise flowers are arranged in tubes of water concealed behind the interestingly textured driftwood.

Some cultural hints

This plant arrangement has been thriving for several years and consists of ivy, palm, variegated aspidistra and *Jasminum polyanthum* growing over old vine branches. The secret of preservation lies in the watering. This type of culture is without drainage which means that watering must not exceed the day to day requirements of the plants. It is difficult to generalize, but one to two cups of water per week are ample for a medium sized decoration. Inspection of the sub-soil will soon show if stagnant conditions exist. Do not use soil for planting, other than the soil contained in the root ball, packing moss tightly around each item. I use only sphagnum moss because it grows in boggy places and never smells even if saturated. This particular moss is bright green when growing and dries to resemble natural wool, quickly reabsorbing and retaining moisture when dampened.

A spring garden

In a warm and sunny room; or with the aid of a greenhouse, it is possible to force into bloom early flowering trees and shrubs as well as bulbous subjects, thus widening the range of plants suitable for inclusion in plant arrangements.

The large scale of this decoration may be judged by the hyacinths nestling at the base of the hybrid *Azalea mollis*. Its pink tinted flower buds are opening to display creamy peach throats, filling the room with a honeysuckle scent. The fibrous root system was carefully lifted from the soil prior to forcing and wrapped in sacking so that it can be easily replanted after flowering. It stands in a large copper pan together with a clump of *Bergenia cordifolia*, with mauvish pink flowers, and three purple hyacinths 'Amethyst', all firmly packed with damp moss. The dainty white flowers of narcissi 'Thalia' are cut from the garden and arranged in concealed tubes of water to increase the naturalistic effect.

On a pedestal

Of all the many flowers suitable for combination with plants, lilies excel. They are frequently difficult to place in mixed arrangements of flowers, but set amidst a bowl of plants in a tube of water they can rise stately and serene above the herbage, rather as they do in the garden. To arrange a flower as it grows is usually the happiest solution indoors, but we can never hope to achieve the casual grace of nature.

Plants are gregarious creatures and flourish when grouped together in communities. Here *Begonia masoniana* (Iron Cross), croton and crinkle-leafed *Peperomia hederæfolia* foil the sacred lily of Japan, *Lilium auratum*. The trailing nepeta carries the eye downwards to the carved capital of the plinth supporting this Warwick vase. The reflexed petals of the lilies echo the architectural curves of the stylized acanthus leaves on the column, helping to give a satisfying unity to the composition.

The Manor House, Heslington

Lady Deramore is an enthusiastic gardener and grows all the plant material used in the exquisite dried arrangements for which she is justly noted. Her elegant drawing room is planned to create a harmonious background, with its monochromatic scheme of aqueous grey-blue, for the many family portraits, landscapes and flower paintings of the Dutch school from ancestral Heslington Hall. Cushions, pictures and flowers are used to introduce unusual touches of colour within this tranquil setting.

My plant arrangement attempts to repeat and blend with these colours. A slender eucalyptus captures this elusive tone of grey balanced by the trailing *Helichrysum petiolatum* and echoed by the cyclamen, *Begonia rex* and downy succulent, all varied in their form and texture. Two gaily coloured crotons pick up the coral and creams of the silk cushions together with three rose beige rayonante chrysanthemums. The latter are kept fresh along with some glaucous cabbage leaves in jars of water concealed amidst the plants.

Grandmother's work-box

A Victorian work-box lined with a pie dish houses this flourishing group of plants established for three years in these confined quarters. The secret lies in selecting plants with the same cultural requirements. The following are from my experience the toughest of indoor plants. To the lower left is the kangaroo vine, *Cissus antarctica*, and above this the once despised, now much prized, variegated aspidistra. Curving height and trails are supplied by *Rhoicissus rhomboidea*, a most accommodating climber. Most palms are extremely hard wearing and *Neanthe bella* on the right never outgrows its welcome in my mixed bowls. All these are shade-loving and get a shampoo of tepid water when time permits. Cream roses in test tubes are used here to spruce up its appearance, but I think bulbous subjects look the most convincing in this type of harmless deception.

A dish garden

Dish gardens bring to mind childhood efforts with bits and pieces frequently ill-suited for combination. Let one plant dominate the scene and a choice of companions will quickly suggest themselves to the arranger's eye, governed by what is available. This striking *Begonia rex* of wine and silver immediately called to mind an old pewter dish and then followed a trailing ivy, *Hedera helix lutzii* and the purple and silver tradescantia. The gnarled root of weathered wood adds interest to the medley of greys and plum pinks, strengthened by three grey-green succulents at the focal area. Some delicately fashioned nerines of clear sugar pink have an almost iridescent quality of petal and supply a lovely touch of autumn colour. Placed on a small chest the finished garden will last for several weeks before the plants are eventually repotted and returned to the greenhouse.

Dried decorations

Though nothing can bring back the hour
Of splendour in the grass, of glory in the flower,
We will grieve not, rather find
Strength in what remains behind.
WILLIAM WORDSWORTH

Of the many types of decorations I have described, dried ones are among my favourites. The reason for this is twofold. First, their subdued colouring holds immense appeal making one more fully conscious of the fascination of texture and form, qualities sometimes missed when colouring predominates. Secondly, because the labour involved in creating any floral arrangement is considerable and in the case of dried arrangement the finished effect can be enjoyed for a much longer period and without further attention.

Here we see a dried arrangement bathed in autumn sunshine in a room ideally suited to its muted tones of orange, tan and parchment yellow.

The container is a copper samovar and forms the centrepiece of a green leather-topped rent table. The coral red curtain pelmets and carpet make a vibrant foil for this all round decoration of seedheads, leaves and flowers firmly fixed into a polystyrene foundation.

134

A library wheelbarrow

This Regency library wheelbarrow makes an original holder for assorted dried seedheads and leaves. Forming an eye-catching decoration for a large entrance hall, it brings a touch of the garden into the house.

The barrow, once used for heavy books, is beautifully bound with brass and inlaid with olive-green leather. The colours of the wood and leather influenced the choice of ornamental sweet corn cobs and dried green hydrangea heads. Tall spikes of imported verbascum link the eye to the staircase beyond. Other outline material consists of dark brown cycas palms and broad ti leaves, both glycerined and pliable. Some sprays of orange skeletonized leaves give a rhythmic feeling to the arrangement and contrast with the varied tints of green, cream and brown. All these items are secured in several blocks of dry 'Oasis' covered with wire netting for extra strength.

Shades of horn and leather

These dried arrangements are all without water and this gives scope for the use of unusual yet porous containers. The coiled ram's horn mounted with silver was originally intended as a communal snuff box and now holds a decoration secured in clay.

Velvety brown reedmace (*Typha latifolia*) and the rounded seedheads of wild onion lead the eye to three seed pods of Hawaiian wood rose. The focal blossom of South African protea is of the same snuff-brown as the horn and is surrounded by feathery petals tipped with reddish brown. Radiating from this point are the furled feather-like spore fronds of the shuttle-cock or ostrich fern, *Matteuca struthiopteris*, a hardy fern. Smooth leathery-textured leaves foil these items, including dark-brown fatsia and honey-yellow aspidistra, both previously given a lengthy glycerine treatment. A touch of delicacy is supplied by wired sprays of skeletonized magnolia leaves dyed to a soft burgundy red.

An everlasting garland

Working with dried materials does not limit the arranger to conventional containers or designs. Here we see a decorative assembly resembling a carved wooden swag or garland. The seventeenth-century carver, Grinling Gibbons, has left a wealth of exquisite examples which can be a constant source of inspiration.

The construction of this type of wall hanging demands patience as well as skill at wiring and mounting each item before assembly on a metal rod. All wires must be covered with florist's plastic self-adhesive tape. Those who have not attempted to make a garland before would be well advised to tackle something simple first, gradually working up to more elaborate designs and I recommend choosing contrasting forms, textures and colours—in that order.

Such mementoes of halcyon days were frequently tied up with ribbons and clutched by cupids. In the same way I tried to work in loops of palm and aspidistra to bind up this garland, which hangs on an overmantel of waxed pine at York Gate, Adel.

Embroidery

This oval panel of moss–green velvet could be used as a decorative wall plaque. The foundation consists of composition board covered with upholstery velvet. The plant material has been chosen with restraint, in an attempt to produce a decoration with all the delicacy of embroidery. The subtle colour scheme of cream, olive green, dull pink and ginger is accentuated by a few glass artificial grapes and the withered black berries of *Hypericum patulum* 'Hidcote' tied up with ecru velvet ribbon.

To succeed with dried arrangements it seems that one must have the habits of a squirrel, hoarding any interesting bits and pieces that may come in useful. This design relies on what was left out rather than what was put in. Each placement was carefully integrated and no strident notes were allowed to creep in. Observe how the areas of plain velvet give value to the off-centre placement of the plant material all of which was wired and pinned to the background.

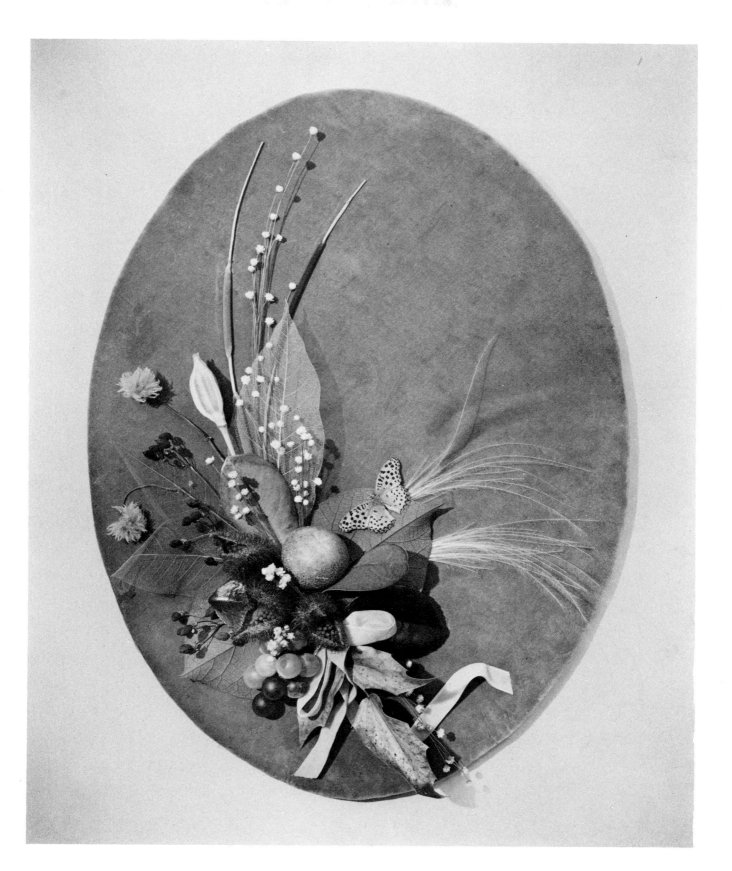

In the formal style

Designed for a traditional setting, this formal arrangement of imposing proportions stands on a vase of milky-pink marble which possesses pleasing shape and sufficient weight to balance the decoration.

An outline of pink-brown eucalyptus and dried pussy willow lead upwards to sedges, hosta seeds and slender reedmace backed by cycas palms. The focal placement of dark brown lotus pods contrasts with two heads of sweet corn. Heart-shaped hau leaves were tinted a pinky red to tone with the marble. This type of decoration could make a permanent display in a room of any temperature. Blowing over it occasionally will remove surface dust, and steaming over a kettle will help to freshen it.

Excellent results can now be achieved with flowers dried in a proprietary brand of powder, but for my own part, I prefer the fruition of seedheads, grasses and leaves which have none of the mummified appearance of home-cured out-of-season blooms.

In the modern manner

This design relies on lines and sharp silhouettes rather than massed materials. The colouring of cream, pinky red and black is enhanced by the sand-blasted branches of manzanita—a particularly durable type of desert wood. The creamy pom-poms are the central boss of seeds from cardoon heads and these have been specially treated so that they cannot disintegrate. Curved and looped ti leaves of smooth texture and greenish-black colouring provide a sharp contrast. As a counterbalance to the asymmetry of the design three reddish hau leaves are placed low down to the left, the colour of these leaves is taken up by the preserved sprays of eucalyptus foliage which form the outline of the composition. The container is an oval black bowl which has been set on a woven straw cloth tray. All these materials are available at florists and will last indefinitely.

A doll's carriage
at Leathley Hall

When unconventional containers are used for flowers the effect is sometimes as incongruous as painted gnomes or silver balls in a garden. Happily this leatherbound and iron-shod doll's bath chair is so finely made and has such a mellow patina that it is well suited as a container, and looks particularly attractive with dried flowers and leaves. Decorative ideas such as this and other examples on these pages are merely suggestions to be adapted for personal tastes and needs in different settings and countries.

Leathley's hostess, busy with a young family, staff and entertaining has solved her decorative problems by using an underlying theme of my dried arrangements throughout the house. These supply the essential feeling real flowers give to a home without the labour involved in their maintenance.

Christmas decorations

At Christmas I no more desire a rose
Than wish a snow in May's new-fangled mirth;
But like of each thing that in season grows.
WILLIAM SHAKESPEARE

Festive decorations form an important part of every flower arranger's calendar and at Christmas they have come to include a catholic assortment of real and artificial material. As a result of seasonal scarcity we often permit ourselves to use a sham leaf or flower to brighten the traditional greenery. However, throughout this book, all the plant material is real except where specifically stated to the contrary.

This simple composition contains cheerful French anemones and mixed evergreens. They are arranged to embrace and enhance an old brass candle lantern which looks as if it belonged in a cattle shed. The welcoming flame symbolizes the coming of Light at the Nativity. A few slender reedmace and ever-green leaves of *Iris foetidissima variegata* add height to the golden yew, variegated holly and ivy all placed on a rustic slice of Yule log.

A festive fireplace

The hearth is the traditional centre of the home and it is here that we like to extend a warm welcome to everyone, especially at Christmas time. Overmantels lend themselves to a variety of decorative treatments depending on their character. In this design, the attempt was made to capture something of the formal elegance of the fireplace by using a graceful garland of artificial fruits and fresh evergreens. The curving line of the swag softens the reeded pine and echoes the line of the fretted fender. It is caught up at each side by Regency candlesticks of muttonfat marble holding scarlet candles. These show up well against the grey jute wall covering, and the flickering light enhances the symmetry of the composition. Each gaily-coloured fruit is foiled by holly, pine or fir and all are firmly bound to a sturdy wire foundation. The colour accents of the flower painting are picked out by the apples, lemons, oranges, nuts and cones of the garland which, for safety's sake hangs well above the dancing flames.

Christmas heralds

Christmas evokes memories of childhood anticipations and joys. In this simple design for children a carved wooden angel stands in wonderment as the Christmas roses force their way through the earth. Like the angel, the *Helleborus niger* appears to herald the event of Christmas with its glistening petal-like sepals of purest white and boss of golden stamen. A few sprays of grey-blue *Cedrus atlantica glauca* encircle the flowers, a branch of alder extends the height. The fascinating wine-red catkins pick up the colour of the *Bergenia beesiana* leaves and veined ivy. This little group stands on a base of hand-carved wood, stained with misty tones of blue and wine. Fir cones and grey reindeer moss conceal the metal receptacle containing a pinholder and water.

A topiary tree

The evergreen Christmas tree has its origins in pagan folklore. It can take many forms and this particular example was designed for a sophisticated party setting in a large country house. Rich draperies and a frocked table create an elegant and colourful background at Leathley Hall for the clipped box-wood tree decorated with berry-like baubles.

The tree was constructed with a piece of small mesh wire netting shaped into a cone and lined with thin polythene. The cone was then tightly packed with damp 'Oasis' and then fitted firmly on to an antique gilded urn. Into this foundation small sprigs of box were inserted and then trimmed with scissors to achieve the topiary effect. Other evergreens could be used instead of boxwood. The tree is decorated with small glass baubles on stiff wires. The evergreen will last long after Twelfth Night, and the tree can continue to be used if the baubles are replaced by small heads of spray chrysanthemums. To keep the material fresh, the foundation must of course be kept moist.

A touch of fantasy

Christmas affords a wonderful opportunity to create something special and festive-looking on the dining table. In preparation for this busy season, many hostesses find it convenient to plan a prefabricated decoration of dried and painted material which requires no further attention.

This centrepiece has a touch of fantasy suggested by the world of ballet. Two brilliant scarlet and pink cockatoos perch on a collection of gilded grasses and plastic fern. Scarlet flocked bulrushes give height together with harestail grasses lightly gummed and sprinkled with untarnishable gold glitter powder. The central flowers are made from crinkled metallic foil paper with gold baubles and tinsel which simulate the pistil and stamen of a Christmas rose. The streamers of red velvet could be extended to each place card or a gift if so desired.

Door bow

At Christmas time it is a pleasant idea to extend our welcome beyond the proverbial mat and tie a festive salutation to the door, so that all can share and enjoy it.

The fifteenth-century Florentine family of della Robbia spent their lives creating beautiful ceramic reliefs of fruits and flowers to adorn the great Renaissance churches of Italy. These garlands have been the inspiration for countless copies hung as a welcome on doors all over the world. In this example both artificial and real fruits are wired on to a circular wire frame backed by assorted evergreens. The idea was to include as colourful and varied a selection as possible bearing in mind the possible temptation offered to youthful carol singers and also inclement weather! Tied up with a lavish bow of water-repellent velvet ribbon it manages to survive most vicissitudes until Twelfth Night.

Paint and glitter

The demand for fresh flowers and greenery at Christmas frequently results in high prices. However, with a little ingenuity and imagination many economical yet exciting effects can be accomplished with painted and glittered materials. Fresh green leaves should be prepared first with a sealing agent such as 'Unibond'. They can then be painted. A more even effect can be obtained with paint spray than with brush and if desired two-tone effects can be achieved. Here is an arrangement of seedheads and leaves painted copper and then highlighted with silver. The effect is more striking than can be conveyed in a photograph. The central flowers, reminiscent of poinsettias, are made from silver and copper foil paper petals gummed together and stiffened by a middle rib of wire. Glittered stamens complete the illusion. The intriguing form of lotus pods add interest, backed by bay grape leaves, mahonia, broom and tall leaves of dried *Cotyledon simplicifolia* all fixed in floral clay on a copper tray.

A Christmas candle

A decoration of both real and artificial material plays a subsidiary role grouped around the dominant feature of a Church candlestick selected for its Christmas associations. The fretted design of fleur-de-lys around the brass spikelet's gallery prompted the use of sham lilies of cream and gold. Other imitation flowers include poinsettias made from almond-green flock wallpaper with centres of gilded quaking grass. A few fluffy gold tinsels suggest imaginary seedheads backed by dark bronze imitation poppy leaves. The tulip pods used to point up the outline are real, but have been dried and gilded. Fresh leaves of *Iris foetidissima* and bronze and green ivy unify these items and supply a soothing touch of green, as does the base of olive-green velvet. The candle, which plays an important role in the design, is home-made and some experimenting was needed to produce an attractive apple-green tint.

Modern designs

At last he rose, and twitch'd his mantle blue;
Tomorrow to fresh woods, and pastures new.
JOHN MILTON

Modern arrangements rely more on the use of lines than on mass effects, consequently colour can play a less important role than form and texture. Lines are expressive and can be used to create many different moods and meanings.

This design is composed of Bird of Paradise flowers (*Strelitzia reginae*), and semitropical foliage. The outline is a conventional triangle but the essential design element of space is stressed in a modern manner to give more meaning to each flower and leaf. As a sculptor creates a free three-dimensional study, so flower arrangers try to exploit height, width and depth so that the materials used are displayed to their fullest advantage.

Design with arum lilies

An effective pattern is achieved with the strong curving lines of the lilies arranged in a large, handmade pottery bowl. Plum-red stems of early willow, *Salix daphnoides*, give directional movement away from the focal placement of flowers. A piece of driftwood echoes the sculptured shape of the lily spathes and its opposing curve and rough texture enlivens the overall crescent design. Sturdy *Bergenia cordifolia* leaves add stability and hide the pinholder, their liver-red winter colouring matching the subdued red of the willow stems.

The asymmetry of the design is balanced by placing the bowl to one end of a carved base. The soft earthy colours of the two form a perfect foil for the purity of the flowers. Black ivy berries add interest and help to extend the movement from the willow tips through to the end of the base.

Contrasts

Strongly contrasting forms of plant material have been used to interpret the struggle between good and evil.

Three tall spires of gladioli with fluted petals of lemon yellow create strong vertical lines. The purity of form and upward thrust of the flowers suggest the search for light. The opposing force is indicated by spines of *Aegle sepiaria*, the hardy orange, with its tangled form and dark bitter green colour. Confused crossing lines were introduced into the design to symbolize the conflict between the two forces and the devious paths of evil.

Further contrasts were worked out between the coarse textured base of plaited rushes and the smooth black pottery bowl. One leaf of bergenia anchors the design to the container and conceals the pinholder support.

Simplicity

After creating groups which incorporate many flowers it is a refreshing change to work with one or two perfect blooms. Here two stems of orange lilies are simply arranged in a basket of woven and varnished palm to emulate the serene understated lines of a Chinese etching.

Slender almost tremulous lines of brown-stemmed and green-budded willow draw the eye to the orange flowers with their brown speckles which match the colour of the basket. Their reflexed shining petals harmonize with the shape of the container which in turn balances the off-centre placement of plant material. The basket is fitted with a metal lining and the plant stems are firmly gripped at this angle by means of a forked stick (Kubari) wedged at the rim. Following oriental tradition the basket stands without a base.

The vertical line

Vertical lines, like church spires, are uplifting and aspirational. An example of this visual effect can be seen in plate 85.

In this decoration the vertical movement is strongly defined, but the materials also possess gentle curves which contrast with each other in individual form. Two sprays of spider orchids from Singapore are straw yellow mottled with maroon. These associate beautifully with three honey-beige and wine-pink stalks of ripe sweet corn, reminiscent of bamboo. The broken line of the orchid sprays contrasts with the smooth repetition of the stalks. Contrast of both colour and form comes from grey-green succulents arranged to cascade down the Chinese vase of celadon-green glaze which stands on a burl of oriental polished wood.

Tropicana

In modern flower arrangements, rhythmic movement can be developed and expressed in a number of ways. Previous examples have shown the importance of space as a component of design. In this example, the feeling of movement and space are equally important to the final effect. Spiral swirls made from split palm fronds are bound on to sweet corn stalks with raffia, creating a visually stimulating background for two pink anthuriums. The tight coil of the palm encloses space and this in turn echoes the shape of the rice-winnowing basket of plaited palm.

By the use of overlapping leaves of aspidistra and anthurium, repetition of solid forms adds emphasis to the dramatic movement suggested by the line of the palm. The deep green glossy foliage also provides a strong colour compliment to the pink of the flowers.

Spring song

Three branches of the service tree are sufficient to portray the simple beauty of springtime. By restrained use of materials we become more conscious of each pearly bud as it opens to reveal downy leaves of grey-green perfection. *Sorbus aria lutescens* is a small tree which will enhance any arranger's garden. The gently embracing lines of these three branches borrows much from the art of Japanese flower arrangement as do so many of our modern occidental designs. It requires only three white iris to complete this simple group with a few hosta leaves added for basal weight and finish.

(Plantain lilies are known to every arranger and much prized for their bold foliage and pale lavender to white flowers. This is a particular favourite of mine from amongst the many, *Hosta fortunei albo-picta*, with leaves of acid yellow edged with green which dull in colour as they mature.)

Sea forms

The texture of plant material is one of the most varied and fascinating design elements discussed in this chapter. The range is infinite and combinations of textures add variety and interest to every arrangement. It is by touching, both physically and visually, that we experience and appreciate texture.

Sun-bleached twigs of dead fern gathered on the shores of Ibiza are rough and prickly in appearance and are faintly reminiscent of sea horses. The steely-blue sea holly is linked by form and texture with its inflorescence of spiny bracts. This particular species is *Eryngium giganteum*, or 'Miss Willmott's Ghost' as some gardeners call it.

The container, a beautiful piece of basin coral from the Great Barrier Reef, has a sharp and jagged surface which contrasts with the smooth base of polished mahogany.

Future trends

Art hath an Enemy called ignorance.
BEN JONSON

It is with some trepidation that I attempt to predict what trends will influence the flower arrangements of tomorrow, for many of my readers will not applaud these tendencies or my views. Many who love flowers and gardens will cling to the massed style in the British tradition. However, a small minority are already exploring the visually exciting possibilities offered by abstract expressions, viewing their plant material with the keen eye of the sculptor who seeks an image hidden in the stone. Their efforts are condemned, like all new forms of artistic expression, until overcoming public prejudice they find themselves in vogue and widely copied!

These futuristic designs are a reflection of our times and are tailored to fulfil the requirements of modern settings with the restrictions they impose upon the arranger by fierce lighting, central heating and plain expanses of glass and concrete. To combat these factors we must overhaul our approach to our subject.

This illustration shows two blue umbels of agapanthus with driftwood in a pottery jar on a rough base, forming a bold dynamic design with strong textural interest.

Abstract viewpoint

Abstract designs are still in their infancy in some countries. But elsewhere, where the art of Ikebana has had a longer appreciation and greater influence, arrangers have learned to accept and understand designs of plant material which bear no apparent bearing on nature and natural growth. Clipping, distorting and painting of plant material are accepted without a second glance, while in more conservative circles even a dyed leaf is enough to make the tinted hair of the judge stand on end! It is unfortunate that we are so quick to lay down arbitrary regulations for others. Some may not choose to gild the lily, but at least should bear with others with differing tastes.

Four leaves of clipped palmetto palm create a radiating framework for one exotic banana flower of maroon and grey. The accordion-pleated leaves create an interesting corrugated surface over which light and shadow play their own dramatic roles.

Solids and voids

Space becomes one of the most important elements in abstract design, helping to counter-balance the weight of solid objects. Three stems of willow are contorted to enclose space and this gives fuller value to their placement. Two lilac rayonante chrysanthemums contrast in form with the smooth surface of one tan rhododendron leaf. The container, of my own design, was inspired by half a melon. The exterior finish is mat and simulates the surface texture of melon skin whilst inside the shiny glaze is golden green, toning with the willow wands in colour and texture.

A scroll of black lacquered wood sets off the design by supplying a strong colour contrast to the golden green of the container and the lilac of the flowers. This outline material could form the silhouette for any flowers of bold character and would come to life under the dramatic spot lighting frequently used in modern public buildings.

Introspect

Three upward-curving leaves of aspidistra echo the tripod feet of another of my pottery designs for the avant-garde. Two peach roses are framed in a cradle of bleached and orange-tinted wisteria vines. Only the minimum of material is used to make us more fully aware of the perfection of the roses and to avoid detracting from the elongated oval outline of the design set against the triangular container of black and turquoise. The curly knots of wisteria repeat in open forms the solid shape of the overlapping rose petals, bringing to bear a unity of form between otherwise unrelated material.

Much of the third dimension is lost by photography, but this depth plays an important part in these modern expressions. The viewer is taken into the decoration to discover something of himself and of the personality of the arranger, which presents another intriguing facet of abstract trends—the contemplative self analytical aspect.

Sculpture

Modern and classical sculpture offers much to inspire and stimulate the flower arranger's creative urge. How often do we find in nature interesting shapes in stones and driftwood that reminds us of the gifted work of artists who create within these media.

Two strong and beautifully formed seedheads of the crown imperial, *Fritillaria imperialis*, make a free-standing natural sculpture. To balance their off-centre placement, two bold curving leaves of agave give contrast of form. The container of modern Japanese pottery has great affinity of shape and colour to the seedheads and picks up the brown barbs on the tough grey-green leaves. This futuristic design of clear-cut proportions would make an interesting study for a modern building. The materials employed are sufficiently durable to withstand the fierce central heating frequently met with in such settings.

Container trends

Present trends indicate that the containers of tomorrow will place a stronger emphasis on bold shapes of free-form outline. Simplification of shape throws textural interest into stronger relief and many hand potters are already using the opportunity this offers to create rough-textured pottery with exciting glazing of glossy depth occasionally coupled with crazed and metallic effects. These coarse-grained pots associate well with abstract designs of rugged masculine appearance.

Other materials offer exciting possibilities. The jewel colour accents of chunky glass or metal containers of copper, polished steel and blackened iron all accord with the buildings of today.

Here shiny pink anthuriums contrast with downy vines of actinidia, looped to repeat in open form the solid flowers. Pitted lava and a smooth aspidistra leaf link the plant material to the pot of grey and lilac glaze, whilst two circular slate bases supply visual balance.

Explosion

Interpretive flower arrangement is a subject I have scarcely mentioned by name, for every arrangement is in some degree interpretive and conveys something of the arranger's personality to the viewer, no matter how much we may wish to disguise this fact. The popular concept of show-bench song titles leaves much to be desired if our art is to be of real value, for far too much emphasis is placed on accessories to bolster up an inadequate knowledge and manipulation of plant material. Let the plant material tell the story, not the ubiquitous impedimenta.

Composed entirely of dead material this dynamic group employs tightly coiled lines and diagonal radiation to convey an impression of explosion. Sinister black cardoon heads burst over massed agave pods crowded around a withered root. The burnished copper bowl, suggesting heat, stands on a tray marking the perimeter of the blast.

The creative search

This abstract design concludes my book with a little sermonizing I hope my readers will forgive. The white lily symbolizes the budding arranger, innocent of eye. The black glass reflects a foundation of past techniques with all its many facets, set on a silver base of knowledge, circular in form like the returning cycle of the seasons. Behind rises the eroded finger of the powerful force that urges us to create. The crossing reedmace are the scarlet darts of conflicting rules holding the arranger captive, but even these are broken.

The moral is to create rather than copy, for by our search for beauty we enrich not only our lives but also those of others. The satisfaction experienced will not be measured by the degree of talent, for both will increase with experience. May I hope that you will derive much pleasure from your search and be well pleased if you discover yourself.

> This bud of love, by Summer's ripening breath
> May prove a beauteous flower when next we meet.
> WILLIAM SHAKESPEARE

Index

199

Acknowledgments

I should like to record my thanks to the many people who have assisted towards the production of this book. In particular, my friend Brian J. Withill for his many helpful suggestions and for typing the text. My special thanks also to Laurence A. Hill and the staff of Warren Jepson and Company, Leeds, for their patient and painstaking photography of all my arrangements with the exception of the Bermudan plates, which were the work of Thomas W. Hall of Hamilton, Bermuda.

Miss Nora Watson of Beckingham has kindly supplied unusual plant material and assisted with its identification. Mr Fred Whitsey has been responsible for checking the plant nomenclature.

The effectiveness of my decorations leans heavily on the beauty of the settings and I am especially grateful to the following people for so kindly granting me permission to use and have photographed their beautiful settings as a background to my flowers:

The Trustees of Beamsley Hospital, Yorkshire

Nina, Lady Deramore, The Manor House, Heslington

The Earl and Countess of Harewood, Harewood House

The Vicar and Churchwardens of St Michael and All Angels Church, Headingley

Mr and Mrs M. Mackintosh, Leathley Hall, Leathley

J. R. G. Marchetti Esq., The Howroyde, Barkisland and Rycliffe House, Ripponden, Halifax

The Earl and Countess of Rosse, Womersley Park, South Yorkshire

Mrs Sybil B. Spencer, York Gate, Adel

Sir Richard and Lady Sykes, Sledmere House, East Yorkshire

Mr and Mrs George E. Wardman, Mount Pleasant, Bermuda

The Dean and Chapter of Westminster Abbey

The Dean and Chapter of York Minster

The Lord Archbishop of York and Mrs Coggan, Bishopthorpe Palace